Stitches from the Yuletide

Stitches from the Yuletide

Hand Embroidery to Celebrate the Season

Kathy Schmitz

Martingale®
Create with Confidence

DEDICATION

To Mrs. Whitaker, my lovely neighbor who taught
me how to embroider when I was six years old

Stitches from the Yuletide:
Hand Embroidery to Celebrate the Season
© 2018 by Kathy Schmitz

Martingale®
19021 120th Ave. NE, Ste. 102
Bothell, WA 98011-9511 USA
ShopMartingale.com

Printed in China
23 22 21 20 19 18   8 7 6 5 4 3 2 1

Library of Congress Cataloging-in-Publication Data is available upon request.

ISBN: 978-1-60468-895-5

MISSION STATEMENT

Dedicated to providing quality products and service to inspire creativity.

CREDITS

PUBLISHER AND
CHIEF VISIONARY OFFICER
Jennifer Erbe Keltner

CONTENT DIRECTOR
Karen Costello Soltys

DESIGN MANAGER
Adrienne Smitke

MANAGING EDITOR
Tina Cook

PRODUCTION MANAGER
Regina Girard

ACQUISITIONS EDITOR
Karen M. Burns

INTERIOR DESIGNER
Angie Hoogensen

TECHNICAL EDITOR
Ellen Pahl

COVER DESIGNER
Kathy Kotomaimoce

COPY EDITOR
Durby Peterson

PHOTOGRAPHER
Brent Kane

ILLUSTRATOR
Anne Larson

Contents

Introduction

I love it when my whole family gathers during the winter holidays. The laughter and food keep us all wanting to stay just a little longer around the dinner table. And when it snows, that makes the festivities more memorable! In Portland, Oregon, we can't count on snow every winter—but when we do get some, it's magical.

When I was eight years old, we had a big snowstorm. I remember it like it was yesterday. All of the neighborhood kids came out to sled and build snowmen. I don't go sledding much anymore, but I still like a good snowstorm. To sit by a fire and work on hand stitching is one of the best ways to enjoy a snow day.

Stitches from the Yuletide is filled with my memories of snowstorms and happy times during family gatherings. Always, whether we were exchanging gifts or sharing a cup of tea, there was a sense of peace. I hope the designs in this book bring a bit of joy and peace to you and your family.

~ Kathy

Baby, It's Cold Outside!

Even snowmen can get cold feet! This little guy doesn't need to worry about frostbite, though. He's tucked into his cozy mitten snowsuit.

FINISHED SIZE
6" DIAMETER

Materials

12" × 12" square of cream print for embroidery
  background

12" × 12" square of lightweight batting

Heavy-duty thread

6" wooden embroidery hoop

Green craft paint and small brush (optional)

Embroidery Floss

*Colors listed below are for Cosmo embroidery floss.
For DMC equivalents, see page 76.*

129 (orange) for nose

311 (brown) for branches

467 (red) for berries, hat, and mitten

600 (black) for eyes and mouth

686 (dark green) for pine needles, shirt, and hands

892 (medium blue-gray) for head

5012 (variegated light green) for scarf and leaves

Embroidering the Design

1 Find the center of the cream square by gently
finger-pressing the square in half vertically and
horizontally.

2 Trace the embroidery pattern on page 11 onto the
cream square, centering the design.

3 Referring to "Embroidery Stitches" on page 77,
use two strands of floss to embroider the design,
following the embroidery key next to the pattern.

4 When the embroidery is complete, press well.

4 Thread a needle with heavy-duty thread and sew a basting stitch around the circle and batting, about ¼" to ½" from the edge.

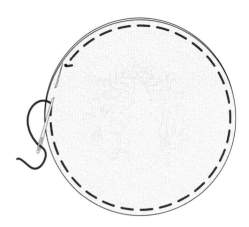

Finishing

1 Paint the outside hoop (the one with the metal attached) if desired. Avoid getting paint on the metal parts. Allow the paint to dry completely.

2 Place the batting on the wrong side of the embroidered piece and quilt as desired. I quilted an outline around all of the embroidery stitching.

3 Press the finished embroidery. Place the inner wooden hoop over the embroidery, keeping the design centered. Trim the background and batting into a circle, 2" beyond the hoop.

5 Place the embroidered and quilted piece over the interior ring of the hoop with the design centered. Secure it in place with the outer hoop. Tighten the screw and adjust the fabric as needed. Draw the ends of the basting stitches to gather the excess fabric on the back. Tie a secure knot.

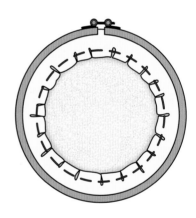

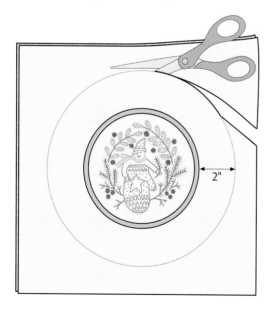

Finishing Touch

For a nicely finished back, cover the stitching with wool. Cut a circle of felted wool the same size as the inner hoop. Position it on the back and sew it to the gathered background fabric with a whipstitch.

Angled blanket stitch

Embroidery key

⌐⌐⌐⌐⌐	Blanket stitch
➤➤➤	Couching
∨	Fly stitch
●	French knot
– – –	Running stitch
▨	Satin stitch
——	Stem stitch
—	Straight stitch

Winter Glory Pillow

When the snowflakes fall, it's time to build a fire and cozy up with this little pillow and a comfy quilt.

FINISHED SIZE
17" × 14"

Materials

Yardage is based on 42"-wide fabric.

14" × 18" rectangle of cream print for embroidery
background

½ yard of green stripe for border and backing

½ yard of muslin or other light fabric for pillow insert

15" × 18" rectangle of lightweight batting

Polyester filling

Cutting

From the green stripe, cut:

2 strips, 2½" × 42"; crosscut into:

    2 strips, 2½" × 14½"

    2 strips, 2½" × 13½"

1 strip, 10½" × 42"; crosscut into 2 rectangles,
    10½" × 14½"

From the muslin, cut:

2 rectangles, 13½" × 16½"

Embroidering the Design

1 Find the center of the cream rectangle by gently
finger-pressing the rectangle in half vertically
and horizontally.

2 Copy or trace the embroidery patterns on pages
15 and 16 onto the cream rectangle and join them
to make a complete pattern. Trace the design,
centering it on the background.

Embroidery Floss

*Colors listed below are for Cosmo embroidery floss.
For DMC equivalents, see page 76.*

129 (orange) for nose

311 (brown) for branches and mouth

467 (red) for holly berries

686 (dark green) for pine needles

775A (gold) for hat and mittens

892 (medium blue-gray) for snowflakes

894 (dark gray-blue) for snowman head,
    eyes, and bird

5012 (variegated light green) for holly leaves
    and buttons on hat and coat

8037 (variegated gold-brown) for coat

3 Referring to "Embroidery Stitches" on page 77, use two strands of floss to embroider the designs, following the embroidery key on page 16.

4 When the embroidery is complete, press well.

Assembling the Pillow

Use a ¼" seam allowance throughout and press the seam allowances toward the darker fabric.

1 Trim the embroidered piece to 13½" × 10½", keeping the design centered.

2 Sew the green 2½" × 13½" border strips to the top and bottom of the embroidered piece and press. Sew the green 2½" × 14½" border strips to the sides. Press.

3 Place the batting on the wrong side of the embroidery and baste. Quilt as desired. I quilted a diamond grid in the background of the embroidered rectangle, with stitching lines ½" apart. Trim the batting even with the pillow front.

4 To make the pillow back, turn under ¼" on one 14½" edge of a green 10½" × 14½" backing rectangle and press. Turn under ¼" again, press, and topstitch. Repeat with the other green rectangle.

5 With right sides together, pin the embroidered pillow front to the backing pieces, overlapping the hemmed edges of the two backing pieces. Keep raw edges aligned. Sew around the outer edges.

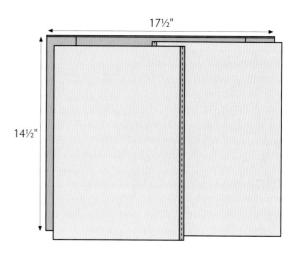

6 Clip the corners, turn the pillow casing right side out, and press. Topstitch ½" from the outer edge of the border strips, overlapping the stitching at the beginning and end.

7 To make the pillow insert, sew the two muslin rectangles right sides together, leaving a 6" opening on one side. Turn right side out. Press the opening edges under ¼". Stuff to the desired plumpness and machine stitch the opening closed.

8 Stuff the pillow insert into the pillow casing through the opening.

Connect on dashed lines to complete pattern.

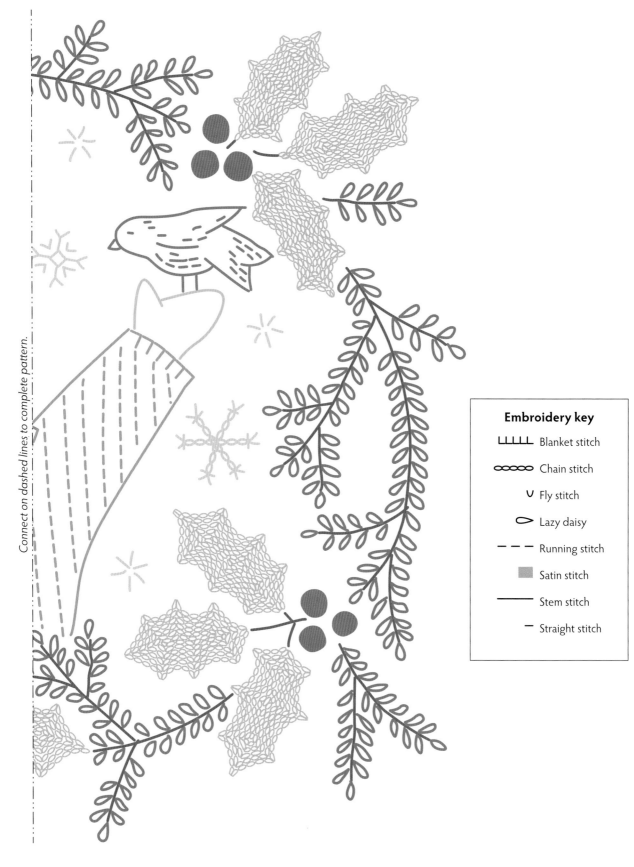

Connect on dashed lines to complete pattern.

Embroidery key

⊥⊥⊥⊥⊥	Blanket stitch
○○○○○	Chain stitch
∨	Fly stitch
⌀	Lazy daisy
– – –	Running stitch
▨	Satin stitch
——	Stem stitch
–	Straight stitch

Winter Fest Table Runner

Dress your table for festive holiday gatherings with this warm and welcoming runner. Just add a yuletide centerpiece to complete your tablescape.

FINISHED SIZE
19" × 37"

Embroidering the Design

1 Find the center of the cream background rectangle by gently finger-pressing the rectangle in half vertically and horizontally.

2 Trace the embroidery pattern on page 21 onto the cream rectangle, repeating it eight times in the positions shown.

Materials

24" × 42" rectangle of cream print for embroidery background

24" × 42" rectangle of light print or solid for backing

24" × 42" rectangle of batting

3 yards of green ¼"-wide rickrack

Embroidery Floss

Colors listed below are for Cosmo embroidery floss. For DMC equivalents, see page 76.

311 (brown) for stems

467 (red) for berries

686 (dark green) for pine branches and needles

8037 (variegated gold-brown) for leaves

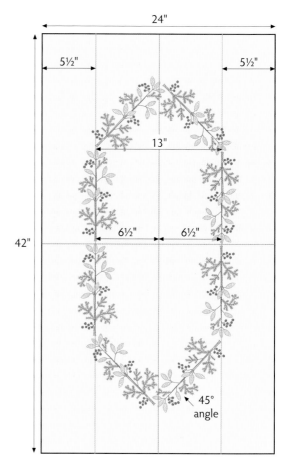

3 Referring to "Embroidery Stitches" on page 77, use two strands of floss to embroider the designs, following the embroidery key next to the pattern.

4 When the embroidery is complete, press well.

Completing the Runner

1 With the design centered, trim the rectangle to 19½" wide. From the center, at the ends, draw a line at a 45° angle, 3¼" from the branches. From the point of the drawn lines, measure in 2½" and draw another line at a 90° angle to the sides as shown in the diagram. Trim off the corners and end triangles.

2 Starting on one of the long sides, place the rickrack parallel to the edge of the fabric as shown, so that you'll stitch through the center of it when sewing a ¼" seam allowance. Leaving a 2" tail, sew the rickrack all around the embroidered top. Overlap the ends ⅛" and then angle them to the outside.

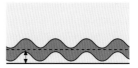

¼" seam allowance

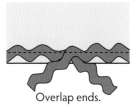

Overlap ends.

3 Cut the backing fabric in half to make two pieces, 21" x 24". With right sides together, sew the two cut pieces together along a 24" edge using a ¼" seam allowance, switching to a basting stitch for 4" at the middle. Press the seam allowances to one side.

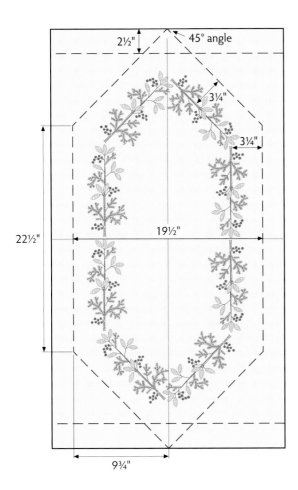

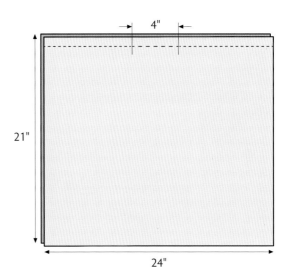

Berry Nice Circles

To add dimension to the berries, adhere fusible web to the wrong side of red fabric scraps and cut circles the same size as the berries. Fuse to the background and satin stitch over the circles.

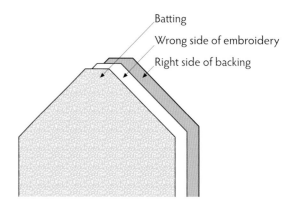

4 Place the batting on the wrong side of the backing. Place the embroidered piece on top, right side facing up. Pin all the way around. Trim the batting and backing to the size and shape of the top.

5 Unpin the stack. With the backing right side up, layer the embroidery, wrong side up, on the backing. Then layer the batting on top.

Batting
Wrong side of embroidery
Right side of backing

6 Pin well and sew around all edges using a ¼" seam allowance. Clip the corners. Remove the basting stitches from the backing and turn the piece right side out through the opening. Press and hand stitch the opening closed.

7 Baste the layers together and quilt as desired. The sample is hand quilted ½" from the outer edges and with a crosshatch pattern spaced 1½" apart, skipping over the embroidery.

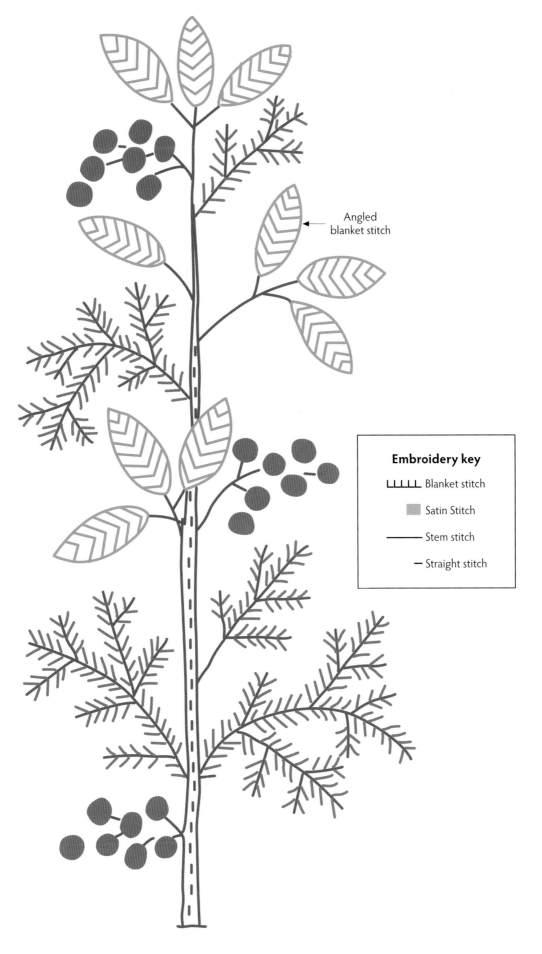

Angled
blanket stitch

Embroidery key

└┴┴┴┴ Blanket stitch

▧ Satin Stitch

— Stem stitch

－ Straight stitch

Frosty-Morning Tea Cozy

Start your frosty mornings with a pot of hot cinnamon-spice tea. Waiting for the tea to steep will be a pleasure with this hand-stitched tea cozy.

FINISHED SIZE
11¾" × 8"

Materials

Yardage is based on 42"-wide fabric.

12" × 16" rectangle of cream print for embroidery background

½ yard of red print for back and lining

¼ yard of green print for binding

12" × 26" rectangle of lightweight batting

10" × 14" rectangle of cardstock for template

Permanent pen or fabric marker

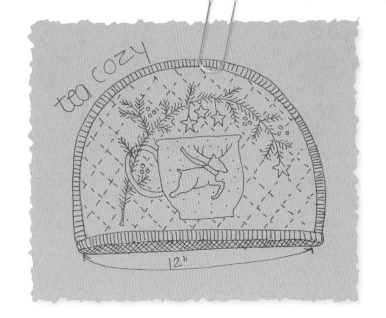

Embroidery Floss

Colors listed below are for Cosmo embroidery floss. For DMC equivalents, see page 76.

311 (brown) for branch and deer

467 (red) for teacup and berries

686 (dark green) for pine needles

775A (gold) for stars

5012 (variegated light green) for scarf

Embroidering the Design

1 Find the center of the cream rectangle by gently finger-pressing the rectangle in half vertically and horizontally.

2 Trace the embroidery pattern on page 25 onto the cream rectangle, centering the design.

3 Referring to "Embroidery Stitches" on page 77, use two strands of floss to embroider the designs, following the embroidery key next to the pattern.

4 When the embroidery is complete, press well.

Cutting

From the red print, cut:
1 strip, 12" × 42"; crosscut into:
   1 rectangle, 12" × 16"
   2 rectangles, 10" × 12"

From the green print, cut:
2 strips, 2½" × 42"

From the batting, cut:
1 rectangle, 12" × 16"
1 rectangle, 10" × 12"

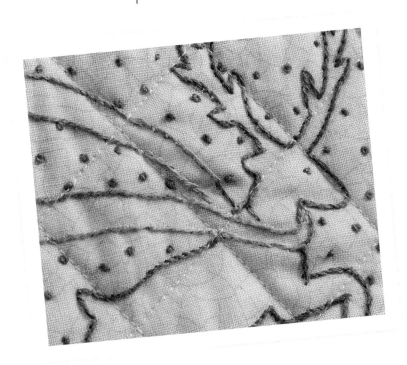

Assembling the Tea Cozy

1 Using the tea cozy pattern on page 26, trace the shape onto the cardstock. Cut along the traced lines to create a "negative" or "window" template.

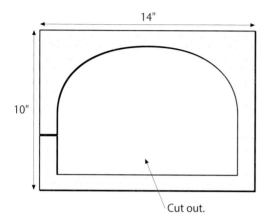

Cut out.

2 Place the template over the embroidery so the design is ½" from the bottom and centered from side to side. Trace the template outline onto the embroidered fabric using a permanent pen. This will be the cutting line after quilting. Repeat to mark the right side of one of the red 10" × 12" rectangles.

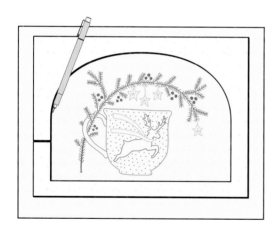

3 Layer and baste the red 12" × 16" lining, the 12" × 16" batting, and the embroidery rectangles together so that the lining and the embroidery are wrong sides together with the batting in between. Layer and baste the two red 10" × 12" rectangles, wrong sides together, with the 10" × 12" batting rectangle in between.

4 Quilt both layered pieces as desired within the drawn outline. The sample is machine quilted with a 1" crosshatch grid.

5 Cut out the quilted pieces along the drawn line.

6 Using a ⅜" seam allowance, sew the front of the tea cozy to the back along the curved edges. The linings should be facing each other.

7 Sew the green 2½"-wide strips together and press in half lengthwise, wrong sides together, to make the binding. Pin and sew the raw edges of the folded binding to the embroidered side of the cozy, using a ⅜" seam allowance. Trim off the excess binding fabric. Fold the folded edge of the binding to the back of the cozy and hand stitch it in place as you would a quilt binding.

8 Sew the remaining binding piece around the bottom of the cozy, starting and stopping along the back. Join the ends; finish as for a quilt binding.

Embroidery key

- French knot
- Lazy daisy
- Satin stitch
- Stem stitch
- Straight stitch

Tea cozy pattern
(one half)

Flip along dashed line to complete the pattern.

With Love Gift Tags

Ribbons and bows are nice, but topping that special gift with one of these handmade gift tags will make your present extra special.

FINISHED SIZE
5¼" × 3"

gift tags with cording ties

Embroidery Floss

Colors listed below are for Cosmo embroidery floss. For DMC equivalents, see page 76.

311 (brown) for branches on Hope tag and leaf stems on Peace tag

467 (red) for ornaments and dots on Joy tag, holly berries and letters on Peace tag

686 (dark green) for letters on Joy tag and small leaf on Hope tag

894 (dark gray-blue) for bird on Hope tag and ornament hook and tie on Joy tag

5012 (variegated light green) for holly leaves and letters on Peace tag

8049 (variegated light blue) for letters on Hope tag and ornament caps on Joy tag

Materials for Three Tags

9" × 15" rectangle of cream print for embroidery background*

3 rectangles, 5" × 9", of light print for backing

9" × 15" rectangle of lightweight batting*

6-strand embroidery floss in 2 different colors for cording**

3 buttons, ½" to ⅝" diameter

Permanent pen or fabric marker

Removable fabric marker

Cord maker (see "Resources" on page 76)

You'll need 1 rectangle, 5" × 9", for each tag.

**Two colors of floss are used for each tag. The Hope tag was made using blue and brown; the other tags were made using red and green. As an alternative to making cording, you can use 2 yards of chenille yarn or other trim.*

Embroidering the Tags

1 Divide the cream rectangle into thirds by gently finger-pressing the 9" × 15" rectangle at the 5" and 10" points.

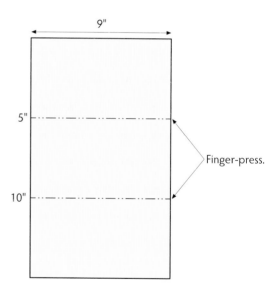

9"

5"

10"

Finger-press.

2 Using a removable fabric marker, trace the embroidery patterns on pages 30 and 31 onto the cream rectangle, centering one in each third of the background. Trace the tag outline using a permanent pen, as this will be the eventual cutting line.

3 Referring to "Embroidery Stitches" on page 77, use two strands of floss to embroider the designs, following the embroidery key next to the patterns.

4 When the embroidery is complete, press well.

Assembling the Gift Tags

1 Place the embroidered piece on top of the batting and baste together. Quilt as desired, keeping the quilting stitches inside the drawn outlines. I quilted an outline next to the embroidery stitching. Cut out the tags on the drawn lines.

2 Using one of the embroidery patterns, trace the tag outline on each 5" × 9" rectangle of backing fabric and cut out on the drawn lines.

3 Pin the backing to the front, right sides together. Sew around the edges using a ¼" seam allowance and leaving a 1½" opening in the middle of the short straight end of the tag for turning. Clip the corners and trim the seam allowances near the corners. Turn the tags right side out. Turn under the edges at the opening and press. Hand stitch the opening closed.

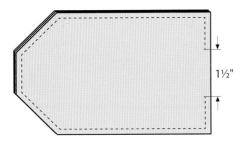

1½"

4 For the cording, cut two 150" lengths of DMC floss, one of each color, and tie the two together at each end to form a loop. Referring to "Cord Making" on page 79, make 28" to 30" of cording using all 12 strands of the floss. Tie the ends and cut off the excess, leaving a ½" fringed tail.

5 Find the center of the cording and pin it to the center of the straight end of the tag. Bring the cording up along the sides to the center of the top of the tag (the angled end). Using one strand of the matching DMC floss, whipstitch the cording in place along the seam. Continue sewing on the cording all around the tag. Tie a square knot where the cording tails meet at the angled end.

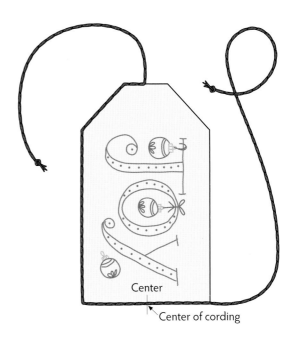

Center

Center of cording

6 Sew the button near the top of the tag, covering the square knot of cording. Use the cording to tie a tag to a special package or to your tree for an ornament.

Embroidery key

⚬⚬⚬⚬⚬ Chain stitch

● French knot

⬯ Lazy daisy

▨ Satin stitch

— Stem stitch

– Straight stitch

Deck the Boughs
Tea Towels

Let the cooking begin! Hand these lovely towels to your kitchen helpers, and drying the dishes will be a pleasure.

FINISHED SIZE
16" x 24"

Materials for One Towel

Towel fabric is 16" wide.

¾ yard of Moda toweling with red stripes (920-130)

Embroidery Floss

Colors listed below are for Cosmo embroidery floss. For DMC equivalents, see page 76.

311 (brown) for branch

467 (red) for ornament

686 (dark green) for pine needles

894 (dark gray-blue) for ornament hanger

Preparing the Towel

1 Trim and square up the ends of the toweling as needed.

2 Turn under ½" on both ends of the toweling and press. Turn under ½" again on both ends and press. Topstitch in place to create the hems.

Embroidering the Design

1 Using the embroidery patterns on pages 34 and 35, trace the chosen design onto the toweling, centered between the red stripes and 2" above the hemmed edge.

2 Referring to "Embroidery Stitches" on page 77, use two strands of floss to embroider the design, following the embroidery key next to the pattern.

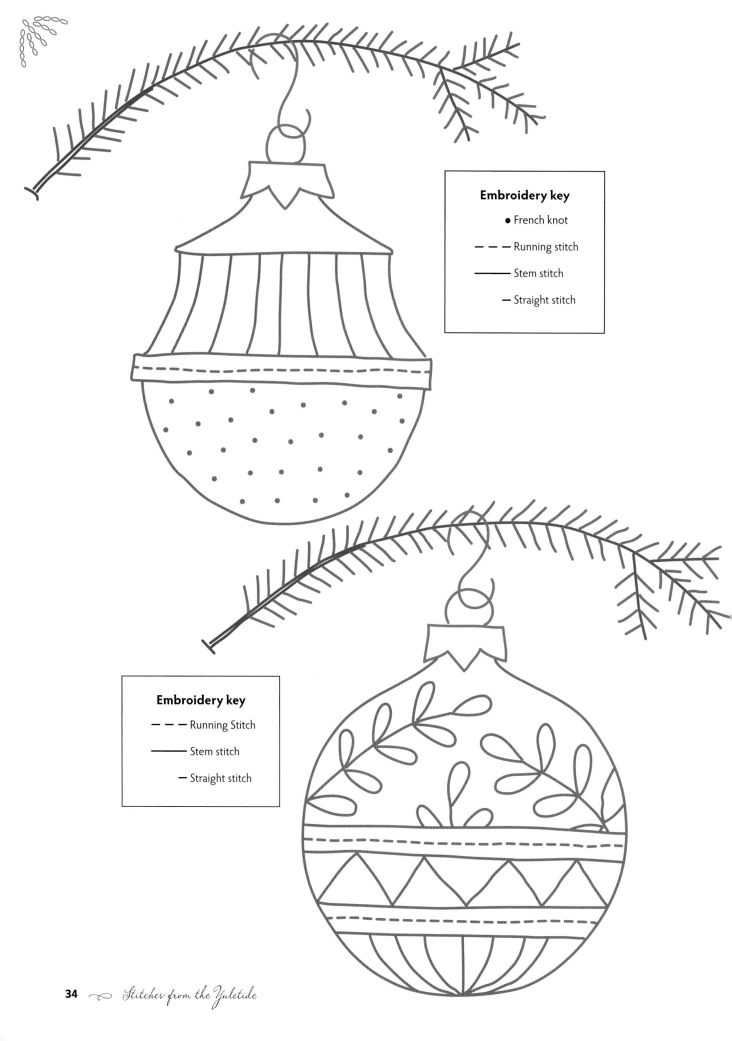

Embroidery key

- • French knot
- - - - Running stitch
- —— Stem stitch
- — Straight stitch

Embroidery key

- - - - Running Stitch
- —— Stem stitch
- — Straight stitch

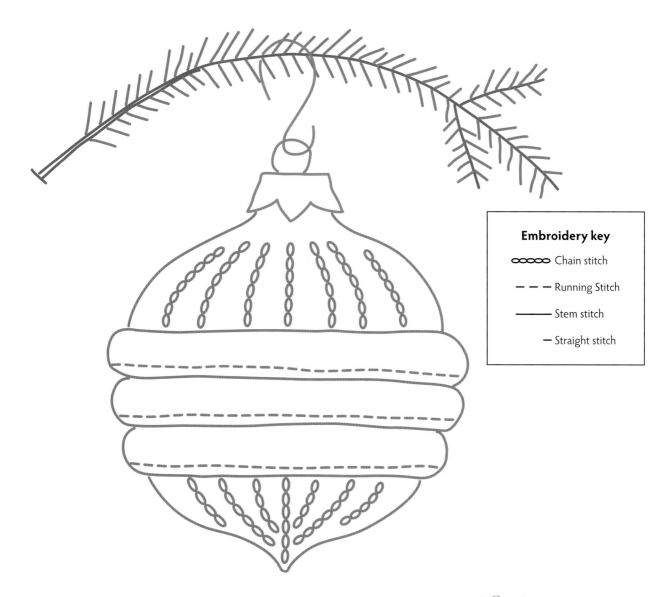

Embroidery key

ᴑᴑᴑᴑᴑ Chain stitch

– – – Running Stitch

— Stem stitch

— Straight stitch

Snow Stitches Needle Book

Every snowflake is unique, just like every stitch you take. Celebrate that special quality with this sweet needle case featuring a single stitched snowflake.

FINISHED SIZE
3" × 4", FOLDED

Materials

7" × 11" rectangle of cream print for embroidery background

7" × 11" rectangle of blue-gray print for lining

3½" × 5" rectangle of blue wool for needle pages

7" × 11" rectangle of lightweight batting

DMC 535 (dark gray) 6-strand embroidery floss for cording*

1 sew-on snap, size 1/0

1 button, ⅝" diameter

Permanent pen or fabric marker

Removable fabric marker

Cord maker*

Pinking shears

*See "Resources" on page 76. As an alternative to making cording, you can use ⅔ yard of chenille yarn or other trim.

Embroidery Floss

Colors listed below are for Cosmo embroidery floss. For DMC equivalents, see page 76.

894 (dark gray-blue) for needle

1000 (ecru) for quilting

8049 (variegated light blue) for snowflake, thread, and needle "holes"

Embroidering the Design

1 Using the pattern on page 39, trace the needle book outline onto the cream rectangle using a permanent pen, as this will be the eventual cutting line. Trace the embroidery design using a removable fabric marker.

2 Referring to "Embroidery Stitches" on page 77, use two strands of floss to embroider the designs, following the embroidery key next to the pattern.

3 When the embroidery is complete, press well.

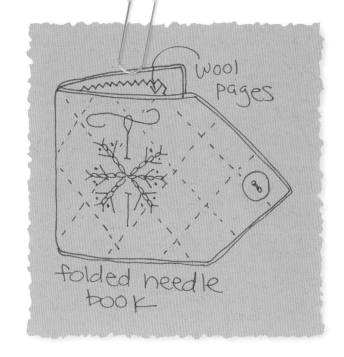

Assembling the Needle Book

1 Trace the diagonal quilting lines onto the embroidered piece using the pattern and a removable fabric marker. You could instead mark the lines with a ruler, spacing them 1" apart.

2 Place the embroidered piece on top of the batting and baste together. Using two strands of the ecru floss, quilt the diagonal grid in the background. Cut out along the drawn outline.

3 Trace the pattern outline onto the lining rectangle and cut out the shape. Pin the lining to the front, right sides together. Sew around the edges using a ¼" seam allowance, leaving a 2" opening at the middle of the short straight end for turning.

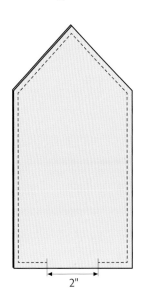

2"

7 For the cording, cut a 120" length of the DMC floss. Referring to "Cord Making" on page 79, make 24" of cording using all six strands of floss.

8 Tuck one tail of the cording inside the opening you used for turning the piece right side out. Use one strand of the DMC floss to whipstitch the cording in place along the seams. When you get back to the opening, tuck the other end of the cording to the inside and then stitch the opening closed.

4 Clip the corners and turn the piece right side out. Press. Press the edges at the opening toward the inside, but *do not* stitch the opening closed yet.

5 Using a pair of pinking shears, trim the edges of the wool on all four sides. Fold the wool in half to measure approximately 2¼" × 3¼" and press.

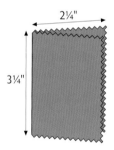

2¼"

3¼"

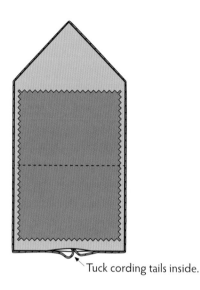

Tuck cording tails inside.

9 Sew half of the snap to the lining, ½" from the point. Sew the button on the other side to cover the snap stitches. Sew the other half of the snap to the outside of the needle book, 1½" from the edge, to complete the needle book.

6 Measure 2¾" from the end with the opening. Align the crease in the wool with this line and pin the wool in place, centered from side to side. Machine stitch through all layers along the crease in the wool.

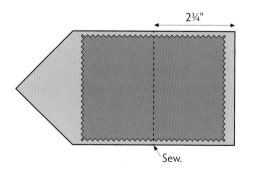

2¾"

Sew.

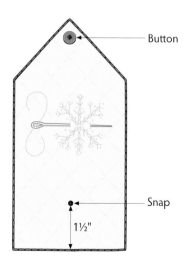

Button

Snap

1½"

4½"

Quilting lines →

Embroidery key

⚭⚭⚭⚭⚭ Chain stitch

• French knot

—— Stem stitch

Cozy Notions Holder

Whenever you want to take your holiday
stitching on the road, grab this handy notions
holder—it's charming and cute too!

FINISHED SIZE
9" × 8", FOLDED

Materials

12" × 20" rectangle of cream print for embroidery background

14" × 30" rectangle of plaid for pocket and handles

12" × 20" rectangle of novelty print for lining

4" × 8" rectangle of charcoal wool for needle book

12" × 20" rectangle of lightweight batting

DMC 535 (dark gray) 6-strand embroidery floss for cording*

2 black sew-on snaps, ½" diameter

4 buttons, ¾" diameter**

Cord maker* (see "Resources" on page 76)

*As an alternative to making cording, you can use 2½ yards of chenille yarn or other trim.

**It's fine (and fun!) to mix and match button sizes and colors.

Embroidery Floss

Colors listed below are for Cosmo floss. For DMC equivalents, see page 76.

129 (orange) for nose

311 (brown) for branches

467 (red) for berries

686 (dark green) for pine needles and shoes

775A (gold) for hat, scarf, mittens, skirt outline and details, and tunic details

892 (medium blue-gray) for lighter snowflakes and chain

894 (dark gray-blue) for darker snowflakes and face

5012 (variegated light green) for tunic

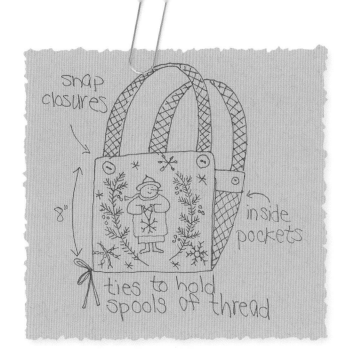

Cutting

From the plaid, cut:
1 rectangle, 9½" × 28½"
2 strips, 3½" × 14"

From the novelty print, cut:
1 rectangle, 9½" × 17"

Embroidering the Design

1 Find the center of the cream rectangle by gently finger-pressing the rectangle in half vertically and horizontally.

2 Trace the embroidery pattern on page 45 onto the cream rectangle, so that the top of the hat is 4" from the top edge of the fabric and the design is centered from side to side.

3 Referring to "Embroidery Stitches" on page 77, use two strands of floss to embroider the designs, following the embroidery key on page 44.

4 When the embroidery is complete, press well.

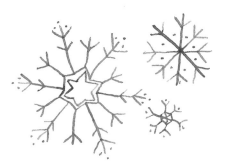

Assembling the Notions Holder

Sew all seams using a ¼" seam allowance.

1 Place the embroidered piece on top of the batting and quilt as desired. I quilted around the embroidery stitches and added small snowflakes in the background.

2 Trim the finished quilted and embroidered piece to 9½" × 17", beginning at the top and centering the design from side to side. The tip of the hat should be 1½" from the top edge when cut.

3 Join the short ends of the plaid 9½" × 28½" pocket fabric with right sides together to form a loop. Press the seam allowances open.

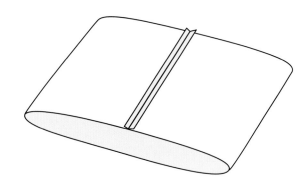

4 Turn the loop right side out and press with the seam centered on one side. Topstitch ¼" from both of the folded edges.

5 To make the handles, fold the plaid 3½" × 14" strips in half, right sides together. Sew along the raw edges of the long side of each to form two tubes. Turn the tubes right side out and press so that the seam runs down the middle. Topstitch ¼" from each long edge.

6 Place the pocket piece, with the seam down, onto the novelty print 9½" × 17" lining rectangle, matching up the sides and centering the pocket from top to bottom. Baste along the long sides using a scant ¼" seam allowance.

9½"

1½"

17"

7 Place the ends of the handles on the right side of the lining, 1" from the sides as shown. The handle seams should be facing up; take care not to twist the handles. Baste the handles in place using a scant ¼" seam allowance.

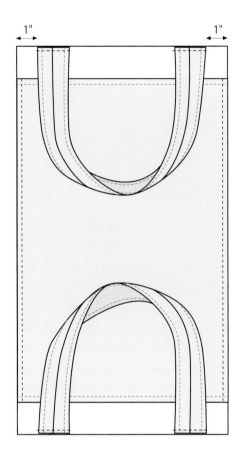

8 Place the embroidered piece, right side down, on top of the lining with the pockets and handles attached, right sides together. Pin and then sew all the way around, leaving a 3" opening along one of the long sides that will be the back of the folder (the half without embroidery).

9 Trim the corners and bulky seams and turn right side out through the opening. Press, turning under the seam allowances at the opening. Don't sew the opening closed yet.

Finishing

1 Fold the piece in half to find the center and lightly press to make a crease. This will be the bottom of the folder. Stitch across from side to side along the crease to form two pockets.

2 For the cording, cut a 270" length of the DMC floss. Referring to "Cord Making" on page 79, make 54" of cording using all six strands of the floss. Tie a knot at both ends.

3 Insert a tail of the cording into the opening on the folder. Using one strand of the same floss, whipstitch the cording in place all around the folder. When you reach the start of the opening, stitch it closed as you also finish sewing on the cording. Tuck the end of the cording inside the opening, overlapping where the cording began so that the ends are hidden.

4 Cut a 175" length of the DMC floss. Make 35" of cording using all six strands of floss. Tie a knot at both ends.

5 Center the wool 4" × 8" rectangle on the interior of the folder. Fold the 35"-long cording in half and place the fold at an edge of the folder as shown. Lay the cording on top of the wool, across the center, covering the width of the folder along the stitched center. Zigzag stitch over one length of the cording from one side of the folder to the other. The stitching should follow the straight-stitched center line.

6 Insert the end of the free length of cording through the center of a spool of thread and tie the ends together to secure the spool in place.

7 Sew the snaps onto the inside top corners of the folder on the lining side. Sew the buttons to the exterior of the folder, on the other side of the snaps, to hide any stitching from the snaps.

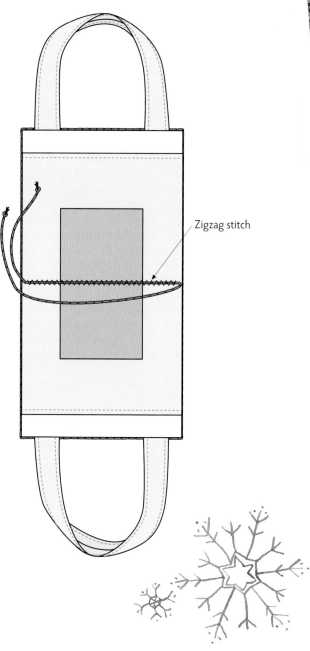

Zigzag stitch

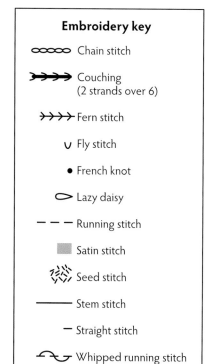

Embroidery key

⧬⧬⧬⧬⧬	Chain stitch
➤➤➤➤	Couching (2 strands over 6)
❯❯❯❯	Fern stitch
∨	Fly stitch
●	French knot
⬯	Lazy daisy
– – –	Running stitch
▦	Satin stitch
ꙮ	Seed stitch
——	Stem stitch
—	Straight stitch
∿	Whipped running stitch

Warm Hands and Hearts

Welcome friends and family with this kindhearted trio. When snowmen gather, it always leads to a good time!

FINISHED SIZE
18" × 16"

Materials

Yardage is based on 42"-wide fabric.

16" × 18" rectangle of cream print for embroidery background

¼ yard of beige print for pieced border

⅛ yard of green print for pieced border

½ yard of green stripe for border and backing

16½" × 18½" rectangle of batting

Embroidery Floss

Colors listed below are for Cosmo embroidery floss. For DMC equivalents, see page 76.

129 (orange) for noses

311 (brown) for mouths

467 (red) for coat and shoes of left snowman; socks, dots, collar button, and berries on hat of middle snowman; scarf, mitten, pants and shoes of right snowman

686 (dark green) for hat, mitten, pants, and pine bough in pocket of left snowman; cuff trim, coat band, dress detail, mitten, and shoes of middle snowman; socks and sweater stripes of right snowman

775A (gold) for hatband, collar, elbow patches, and coat band of middle snowman

892 (medium blue-gray) for birds and snowmen's heads and eyes

5012 (variegated light green) for holly in hat of middle snowman; hat, knee patches, sweater outline, and sweater stripes of right snowman

8037 (variegated gold-brown) for coat and hat of middle snowman

Cutting

From the beige print, cut:

1 strip 3" × 42"; crosscut into 12 squares, 3" × 3"

2 squares, 2½" × 2½"

From the green print, cut:

1 strip, 3" × 42"; crosscut into 12 squares, 3" × 3"

From the green stripe, cut:

1 strip, 9½" × 42"; crosscut into 2 rectangles, 9½" × 16½"

2 strips, 1½" × 42"; crosscut into 4 strips, 1½" × 16½"

1 strip, 2½" × 16½"

Embroidering the Design

1 Find the center of the cream rectangle by gently finger-pressing the rectangle in half vertically and horizontally.

2 Copy or trace the embroidery patterns on pages 50 and 51 and join them. Then trace the design onto the cream rectangle.

3 Referring to "Embroidery Stitches" on page 77, use two strands of floss to embroider the design, following the embroidery key next to the pattern.

4 When the embroidery is complete, press well.

Assembling the Wall Hanging

Use a ¼" seam allowance throughout and press the seam allowances as shown by the arrows in the diagrams.

1 Trim the embroidered piece to 12½" × 10½", centering the design.

2 Draw a diagonal line from corner to corner on the wrong side of the 12 beige 3" squares. Layer each square right sides together with a green 3" square. Sew ¼" from each side of the drawn line, cut on the line, and press to make 24 half-square-triangle units. Trim the units to 2½" square.

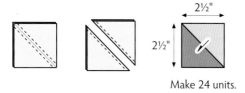

Make 24 units.

3 Sew six half-square-triangle units together to make a row as shown. Make two rows. Make two more rows with the green triangles angled in the direction. Sew a beige 2½" square to one end of two of these rows.

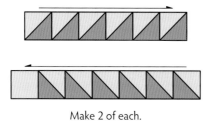

Make 2 of each.

4 Sew the rows with six half-square-triangle units to the top and bottom of the embroidered piece, with the green triangles adjoining the quilt top. Sew the rows with squares to the sides, again sewing the green edges to the quilt.

5 Sew one green stripe 1½" × 16½" strip to the top and one to the bottom of the quilt center. Press the seam allowances toward the green stripe border. Sew the two remaining 1½" × 16½" strips to the sides and press.

Finishing

1 Sew the two green stripe 9½" × 16½" backing rectangles together along the 16½" sides, switching to a basting stitch for 4" in the center. The finished backing piece should measure 16½" × 18½".

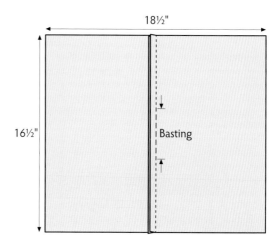

18½"

16½"

Basting

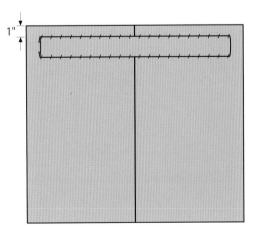

2 Layer the backing and quilt top right sides together.

3 Pin the layers securely and sew around all four edges using a ¼" seam allowance. Clip the corners. Remove the basting stitches from the backing seam and turn the piece right side out through the opening. Press and hand stitch the opening closed.

4 Quilt as desired. The wall hanging shown is machine stitched in the ditch of the pieced borders and free-motion quilted around the embroidery.

5 To make a hanging sleeve, turn under ¼" on all four sides of the green stripe 2½" × 16½" strip and press. Place the sleeve on the back of the project, 1" from the top and centered from side to side. Pin in position and hand stitch along the long sides.

1"

Hand stitch hanging sleeve.

Connect on dashed lines to complete pattern.

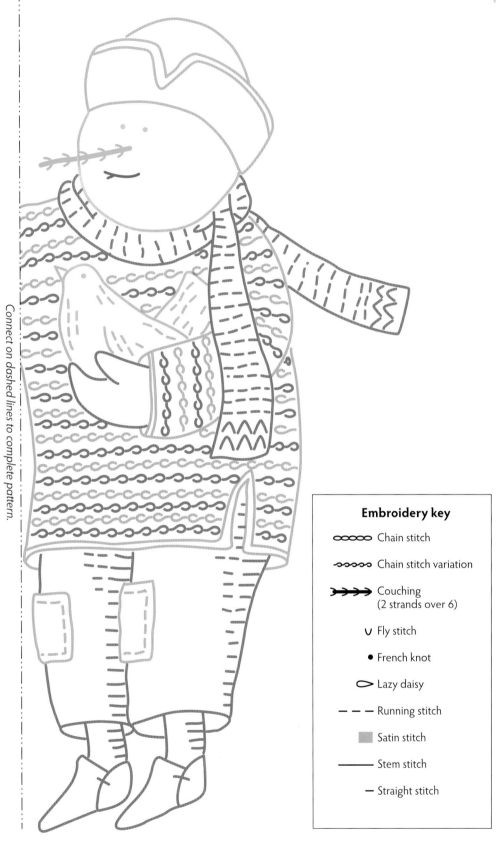

Connect on dashed lines to complete pattern.

Embroidery key

⟨⟨⟨⟨⟨ Chain stitch

⟨⟨⟨⟨⟨ Chain stitch variation

➤➤➤ Couching
(2 strands over 6)

∪ Fly stitch

● French knot

⟨⟩ Lazy daisy

– – – Running stitch

▨ Satin stitch

—— Stem stitch

– Straight stitch

From Me to You Gift-Card Holder

Add handmade charm and a personal touch to monetary gifts with this sweet gift-card holder embellished with holly, berries, and hand quilting.

FINISHED SIZE
3" × 4¼", CLOSED

Materials

6" × 13" rectangle of cream print for embroidery background

3½" × 18" rectangle of red print for lining

6" × 13" rectangle of lightweight batting

1 button with shank, ½" × ⅝" diameter

DMC 3777 (red) 6-strand embroidery floss for cording*

Cord maker (see "Resources" on page 76)

Template plastic

Permanent pen or fabric marker

Removable fabric marker

*As an alternative to making cording, you can use 1 yard of chenille yarn or other trim.

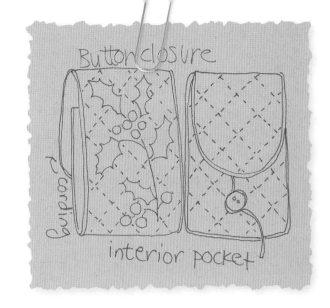

Embroidery Floss

Colors listed below are for Cosmo embroidery floss. For DMC equivalents, see page 76.

467 (red) for holly berries and quilting

5012 (variegated light green) for holly leaves

Embroidering the Design

1 Find the center of the cream rectangle by gently finger-pressing the rectangle in half vertically and horizontally.

2 Trace the embroidery pattern on page 55 onto the cream rectangle, matching up the two parts of the design and centering it on the background. Trace the outline using a permanent pen, as this will be the eventual cutting line. Trace the design using a removable fabric marker.

3 Referring to "Embroidery Stitches" on page 77, use two strands of floss to embroider the designs, following the embroidery key next to the pattern.

4 When the embroidery is complete, press well.

Assembling the Gift-Card Holder

1 Trace the diagonal quilting lines using the pattern on page 55 and a removable fabric marker. You could instead mark the lines with a ruler, spacing them ¾" apart.

2 Place the embroidered piece on top of the batting and baste around the edges. Quilt using two strands of the Cosmo 467 (red) floss along the diamond crosshatch lines. Sew on the button 3½" from the straight end and centered from side to side. Cut out the stitched piece along the drawn outer line.

3 Using the template plastic and permanent pen, trace around the curved end of the embroidery pattern and cut out the shape to make a template. Trace around it on one end of the red print 3½" × 18" lining rectangle and cut a rounded end. From the top of this curve, measure 17" and cut the other end to this length.

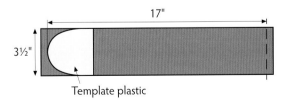

Template plastic

4 Make a fold 7" from the straight end, with wrong sides together, and press. Turn the piece over and bring this fold toward the rounded end until the length measures 11". This will create the pocket for holding a gift card or folded bills.

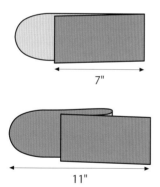

7"

11"

5 Pin the folded lining to the embroidered piece, right sides together, aligning the raw edges. Sew around the edges, leaving a 2" opening at the short straight end for turning. Clip the corners and seam allowances along the curve. Turn the piece right side out and press. Press the edges of the opening under ¼". Hand stitch the opening closed.

2"

6 With the lining together and the fold at the bottom of the pocket, bring the straight end up and press. Fold the curved end down 2½", overlapping the straight end, and press.

7 For the cording, cut a 165" length of the DMC floss. Referring to "Cord Making" on page 79, make 33" of cording using all six strands of the floss.

8 Starting at the center of the curve with the *looped* end of the cording, not the knotted end, use one strand of the DMC floss to whipstitch the cording in place along the edges all the way around. There will be a tail left at the top of the curve. Use this tail to wrap around the button. Trim the tail to the desired length and tie a knot.

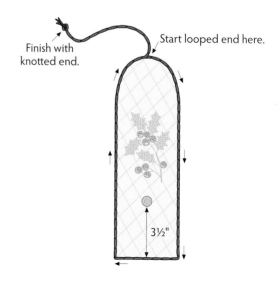

Finish with knotted end.

Start looped end here.

3½"

Top

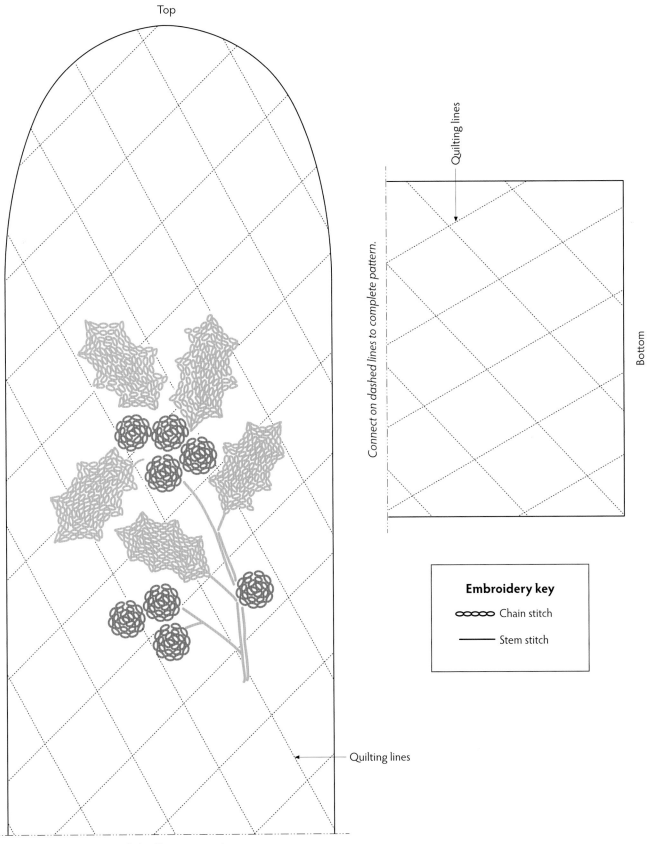

Connect on dashed lines to complete pattern.

Quilting lines

Bottom

Quilting lines

Embroidery key

ᴐᴐᴐᴐᴐ Chain stitch

—— Stem stitch

Connect on dashed lines to complete pattern.

Christmas Cheer Ornaments

Whether you hang them from a tree bough or on a doorknob, these classic ornaments will bring a smile to all.

FINISHED SIZE
2½" DIAMETER

Materials for Four Ornaments

12" × 12" square of cream print for embroidery background

4 squares, 4" × 4", of red or green wool for backing

12" × 12" square of batting

4 Half Ball Cover Buttons (Dritz size 100, 2½" diameter)

DMC 3777 (red) and/or DMC 936 (green) 6-strand embroidery floss for cording*

Cord maker (see "Resources" on page 76)

Permanent pen or fabric marker

Removable fabric marker

White household glue

Pinking shears

As an alternative to making cording, you can use ¾ yard of chenille yarn or other trim.

Embroidery Floss

Colors listed below are for Cosmo embroidery floss. For DMC equivalents, see page 76.

467 (red) for bird, stocking, ornament, and holly berries

686 (dark green) for pine boughs

775A (gold) for star and berries on branches

5012 (variegated light green) for holly leaves, ornament hanger, and branches

Embroidering the Designs

1 Divide the cream square into quarters by gently finger-pressing the square in half vertically and horizontally.

2 Using a removable fabric marker, trace the embroidery patterns on page 59 onto the cream square, centering one pattern in each quarter of the background. Trace the circle outline using a permanent pen, as this will be the eventual cutting line.

3 Referring to "Embroidery Stitches" on page 77, use two strands of floss to embroider the designs, following the embroidery key next to the patterns.

4 When the embroidery is complete, press well.

Assembling the Ornaments

1 Place the embroidered piece on the batting and baste together. Quilt as desired, keeping the stitches within the drawn circles. In the ornaments on page 56, echoing lines are quilted around the embroidered designs.

2 Cut out the embroidered pieces on the drawn circles. Remove the shank from the back of each button blank. Following the manufacturer's instructions, center each ornament on a button blank and secure it in place. Add the metal back.

3 Spread glue on each metal button back. Place a wool square, centered, over the glue on each and set aside to dry. When dry, trim all the way around with pinking shears, leaving ¼" to ⅜" extra all the way around.

small amount of glue around the edge of the button where it meets the wool. Carefully press the cording into the glue. When the two ends of the cording meet at the top of the ornament, tie a square knot and add a touch of glue.

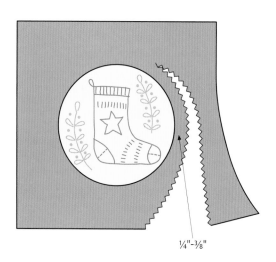

¼"–⅜"

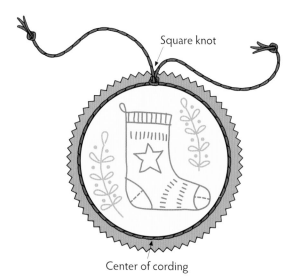

Square knot

Center of cording

4 To make cording, cut a 130" length of the DMC floss for each ornament. Referring to "Cord Making" on page 79, make 26" of cording using all six strands of the floss. Make a knot at both ends and cut off the extra, leaving a ½" fringe.

5 Find the center of the cording and glue it to the bottom center of the ornament with a tiny dot of glue. Using a toothpick or other applicator, spread a

6 Using the cording, tie the ornaments to a tree branch, doorknob, around the neck of a wine bottle, or anywhere else that needs a little yuletide cheer.

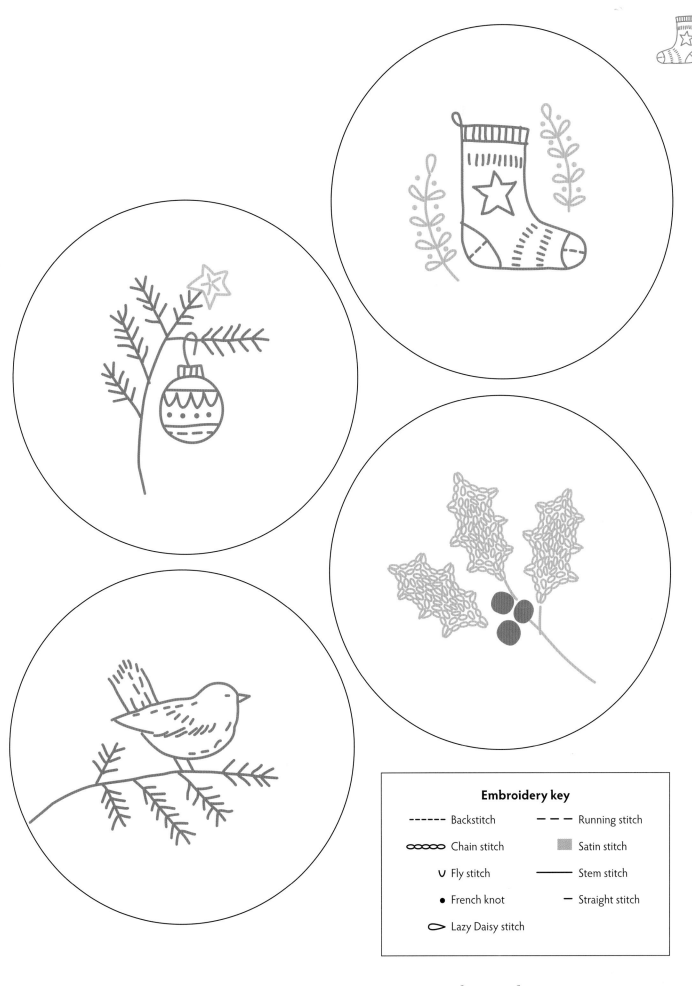

Embroidery key

------- Backstitch   – – – Running stitch

ᴏᴏᴏᴏ Chain stitch   ▨ Satin stitch

ᴠ Fly stitch   —— Stem stitch

• French knot   — Straight stitch

◠ Lazy Daisy stitch

Oh, Deer!

Small enough to hang anywhere yet big enough to hold a special treat, this stocking will deliver Christmas cheer in style.

FINISHED SIZE
9" LONG

Materials

⅓ yard of red print for stocking

5" of fluffy ecru yarn for hanging loop

DMC Ecru 6-strand embroidery floss for cording*

Cord maker (see "Resources" on page 76)

Template plastic

Permanent pen or fabric marker

Marking tool for dark fabric, such as a white Uni-Ball gel pen

As an alternative to making cording, you can use 1 yard of chenille yarn or other trim.

Embroidery Floss

Color listed below is for Cosmo embroidery floss. For DMC equivalent, see page 76.

1000 (ecru) for all stitching

Embroidering the Design

1 Cut the red print into four equal pieces, approximately 10" × 12".

2 Make a template for the stocking using template plastic and the pattern on page 63. Trace the outline of the stocking onto one of the red rectangles using a permanent pen. This will be the cutting line.

3 Trace the embroidery pattern on page 63 inside the stocking outline using the marking tool for dark fabric.

4 Referring to "Embroidery Stitches" on page 77, use two strands of floss and the chain stitch to embroider the designs. Stitch the outlines of the leaves, berries, and deer first; then fill in with chain stitches.

5 When the embroidery is complete, press well.

Assembling the Stocking

1 Layer two of the red 10" × 12" rectangles with wrong sides together. Place the last red 10" × 12" rectangle on top of these, wrong side up.

2 Place the embroidered fabric on top of the stack, right side up, and pin all four pieces together. Carefully cut out the stocking shape on the drawn line through all four layers.

3 Reposition the top two pieces (the embroidered piece and a plain piece) so they are right sides together. Sew the pieces together using a ¼" seam allowance, leaving the top open. Clip and trim the curved seams. Turn the stocking right side out and press.

4 Sew the remaining two stocking pieces right sides together in the same way to make the lining, but leave a 3" opening along the bottom of the stocking for turning. Do not turn right side out.

5 Turn the embroidered stocking wrong side out again. Slip it inside the lining, right sides together, aligning the top edge and matching the side seams. Pin around the top.

6 Fold the fluffy yarn in half to form a loop. Place the loop between the lining and the embroidery, on the heel side of the stocking, leaving 1" of the tails extending above the top.

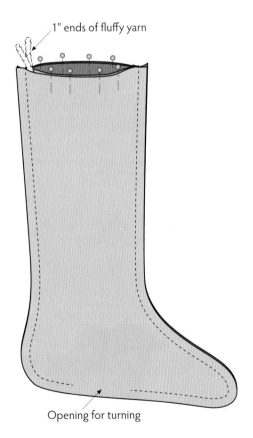

1" ends of fluffy yarn

Opening for turning

7 Using a ¼" seam allowance, sew around the top of the stocking. Turn the stocking right side out through the opening at the bottom of the lining. Hand stitch the opening closed. Slip the lining inside the stocking and press the top seam.

8 For the cording, cut a 5-yard length of the DMC floss. Referring to "Cord Making" on page 79, use all six strands of the floss to make 36" of cording. Tie a knot at the loose end only.

9 Place the unknotted end of the cording at the top of the stocking, on the toe side as shown. Using one strand of the DMC floss, whipstitch the cording in place along the seam, following the direction indicated by the arrows on the diagram. (Work down the front of the stocking first; do the top opening last.) When you get to the opening of the stocking, continue stitching around it also. Tuck any extra cording inside the stocking and tack it in place along the inside seam.

Begin here.

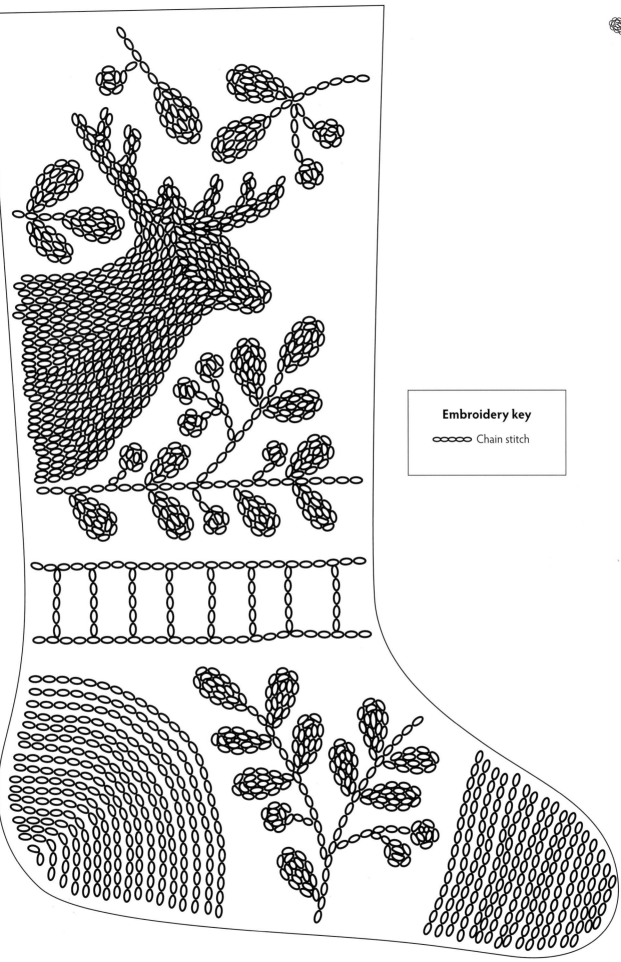

Embroidery key

ᴏᴏᴏᴏᴏ Chain stitch

Giving Tree Tabletop Hanging

Share your joy at Christmas with a stitched display of happy tidings and holiday favorites

FINISHED SIZE
8" × 12½"

Materials

Yardage is based on 42"-wide fabric.

9" × 14" rectangle of cream print for embroidery
   background

⅓ yard of red print for border and backing

8½" × 13" rectangle of batting

6" × 12" Ackfeld wire table stand (optional;
   see "Resources" on page 76)

Embroidery Floss

*Colors listed below are for Cosmo embroidery floss.
For DMC equivalents, see page 76.*

129 (orange) for nose and centers of candle flames

311 (brown) for stems

467 (red) for berries, bird, candy-cane stripes,
   snowman scarf, gift, vase, stocking, and letters

600 (black) for snowman hat, eyes, and mouth

686 (dark green) for pine needles and banner

775A (gold) for stars and candle flames

892 (medium blue-gray) for snowflakes, candles,
   snowman, and ornament

894 (dark gray-blue) for banner ties, ornament
   bows, and candy-cane outline

5012 (variegated light green) for small leaves,
   holly, and leaf in bird's beak

Cutting

From the red print, cut:

2 strips, 1" × 42"; crosscut into:*

   2 strips, 1" × 12"

   2 strips, 1" × 8½"

2 rectangles, 6¾" × 8½"

1 rectangle, 2½" × 7"

*If the strip is at least 41" long after prewashing
and removing selvages, 1 strip will be enough.*

Embroidering the Design

1 Find the center of the cream rectangle by
   gently finger-pressing the rectangle in half
vertically and horizontally.

2 Overlap and align the two parts of the
   embroidery pattern on pages 67 and 68,
and trace the design onto the cream rectangle,
centering it on the background.

3 Referring to "Embroidery Stitches" on page 77,
   use two strands of floss to embroider the
designs, following the embroidery key next to the
bottom pattern.

4 When the embroidery is complete, press well.

Assembling the Tabletop Hanging

Sew all seams with a ¼" seam allowance and press as shown by the arrows in the diagram.

1 Trim the embroidered piece to 7½" × 12", keeping the design centered.

2 Sew the red print 1" × 12" strips to the sides of the embroidered piece. Sew the red print 1" × 8½" strips to the top and bottom.

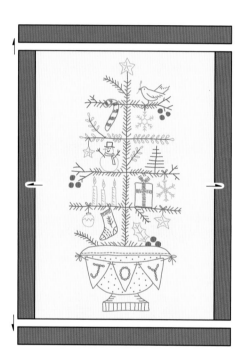

3 Sew the two red 6¾" × 8½" backing rectangles together along the 8½" side, switching to a basting stitch for 3" in the middle. Press the seam allowances to one side. The backing should measure 8½" × 13".

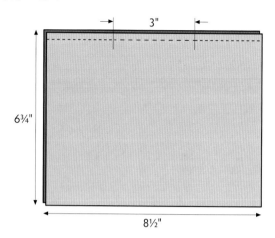

4 Place the backing and embroidered piece right sides together. Layer the batting on top of the embroidery. Pin well and sew around all edges. Clip the corners. Remove the basting stitches from the backing and turn the piece right side out through the opening. Press and hand stitch the opening closed.

5 Hand quilt as desired. The hanging shown is hand quilted with a diagonal crosshatch, with stitching lines 1" apart.

6 To make the hanging sleeve, turn under ¼" on all edges of the red 2½" × 7" rectangle and press. Pin the sleeve 1" from the top of the back, right side up, centering it from side to side. Hand stitch in place along the two long sides.

7 Insert the wire frame into the sleeve.

JOY

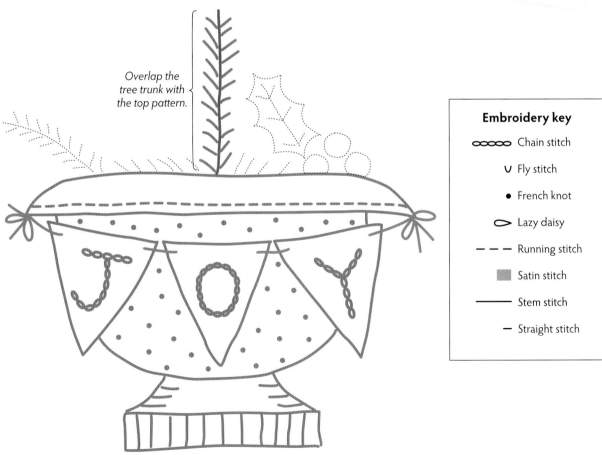

Overlap the tree trunk with the top pattern.
JOY

Bottom pattern

Embroidery key

- Chain stitch
- Fly stitch
- French knot
- Lazy daisy
- Running stitch
- Satin stitch
- Stem stitch
- Straight stitch

*Overlap the tree trunk with
the bottom pattern.*

Top pattern

Bunny Hop Sachet

Dressed for a romp in the snow, this little bunny hops along atop a lavender-filled sachet. Tuck the sachet into any nook, cranny, or drawer to add the sweet scent of summer all winter long.

FINISHED SIZE
5" × 3½"

Materials

6" × 8" rectangle of cream print for embroidery background

6" × 8" rectangle of muslin or other light fabric for sachet insert

6" × 10" rectangle of fabric for backing

6" × 8" rectangle of lightweight batting

½ to ¾ cup of dried lavender flowers for filling

Cutting

From the muslin, cut:
2 rectangles, 3¾" × 5¼"

From the fabric for backing, cut:
2 squares, 4" × 4"

Embroidery Floss

Color listed below is for Cosmo embroidery floss. For DMC equivalent, see page 76. Note that this thread is highly variegated and the color ranges from light brown to blue.

8049 (variegated light blue)

Embroidering the Design

1 Find the center of the cream rectangle by gently finger-pressing the rectangle in half vertically and horizontally.

2 Trace the embroidery pattern on page 71 onto the cream rectangle, centering it.

3 Referring to "Embroidery Stitches" on page 77, use two strands of floss to embroider the design following the embroidery key next to the pattern.

4 When the embroidery is complete, press well.

Assembling the Sachet

1 Place the batting on the wrong side of the embroidered piece and quilt as desired. The sachet shown is echo quilted around the rabbit and randomly throughout the background area.

2 Trim the piece to 4" × 5½", keeping the design centered.

3 Turn under ¼" on one side of each 4" square of backing fabric and press. Turn under ¼" again and press. Topstitch to create hems for the backing pieces.

4 With right sides together, place a backing rectangle on the embroidered piece, aligning the raw edges. Add the second backing rectangle with the wrong side up, aligning the raw edges and overlapping the hemmed edges of the other backing piece. Pin in place. Sew around the four sides using a ¼" seam allowance. Clip the corners. Turn right side out and press.

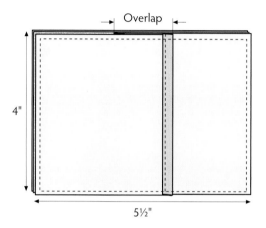

5 Place the muslin rectangles right sides together and sew three sides, leaving one short end open. Turn right side out. Turn under ¼" at the opening and press. Fill with lavender and then machine stitch the opening closed.

6 Insert the lavender-filled pouch into the embroidered casing through the opening in the back.

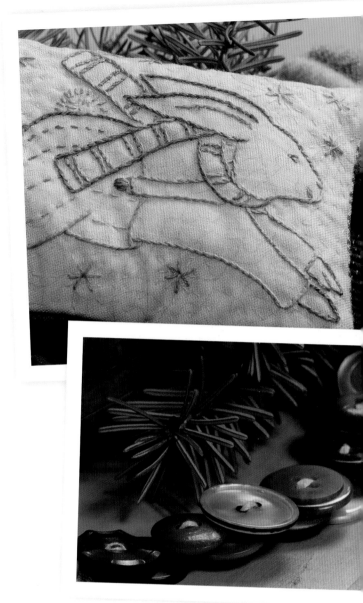

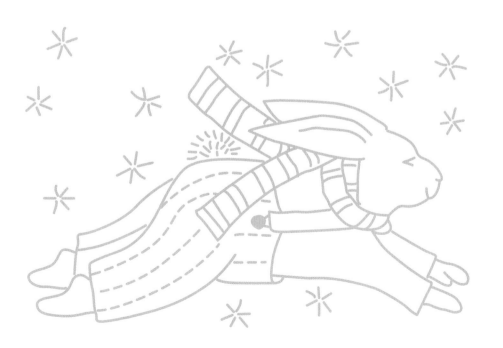

Embroidery key	
– – –	Running stitch
▨	Satin stitch
🧵	Seed stitch
——	Stem stitch
–	Straight stitch

Snow Friends Wall Art

Nothing makes a snow couple happier than sharing a good snowfall with feathered friends.

FINISHED SIZE
10" × 8", EXCLUDING FRAME

Materials

12" × 14" rectangle of cream print for embroidery background

12" × 14" rectangle of lightweight batting

8" × 10" wooden frame with 7⅝" × 9⅝" opening*

Archival tape for securing embroidery in frame

Brads for securing frame backing (optional; see step 3 of "Finishing," below right)

*If the frame doesn't come with cardboard, you'll need two 8" × 10" pieces of cardboard. The embroidered fabric will be wrapped around one piece, and the other will be used as a backing. Using an acid-free board will add to the longevity of your embroidered piece.

Embroidery Floss

Colors listed below are for Cosmo embroidery floss. For DMC equivalents, see page 76.

129 (orange) for noses

311 (brown) for sticks and bird

686 (dark green) for shoes, mittens, and hats

894 (dark gray-blue) for string, banner, and heads

5012 (variegated light green) for pants and dress

8037 (variegated gold-brown) for coats

8049 (variegated light blue) for snowflakes*

*Note that this thread is highly variegated and the color ranges from light brown to blue.

Embroidering the Design

1 Find the center of the cream rectangle by gently finger-pressing the rectangle in half vertically and horizontally.

2 Trace the embroidery pattern on page 74 onto the cream rectangle, centering the design.

3 Referring to "Embroidery Stitches" on page 77, use two strands of floss to embroider the designs, following the embroidery key next to the pattern.

4 When the embroidery is complete, press well.

Finishing

1 Place the batting on the wrong side of the embroidered piece. Add quilting stitches as desired. The wall art on page 72 is quilted around the embroidery elements and with small snowflakes in the background. Curvy quilting lines near the feet depict snow.

2 Trim the batting to 8" × 10" to reduce bulk. Center the piece on the 8" × 10" backing board that came with the frame. Fold the edges of the fabric over the cardboard, making sure the fabric is taut but not distorted. Secure the fabric and batting with archival tape.

3 Cover the back of the project with a second piece of cardboard. Insert the embroidered piece into the frame and secure with the clips that came with the frame or use small brads.

Embroidery key

Couching
(2 strands over 6)

• French knot

⌒ French knot

— — — Running stitch

— Stem stitch

— Straight stitch

Embroidery Basics

In this section, you'll find all you need to get started with hand embroidery. If you're new to sewing and quilting, you can find additional helpful information at ShopMartingale.com/HowtoQuilt, where you can download free illustrated how-to guides on everything from rotary cutting to binding a quilt.

Quilt as Desired

I find it easiest to quilt through as few layers as possible, so I don't put a backing fabric under the batting. I never use a hoop, but I do baste the batting and embroidered piece together well. If it's a small project, I just baste around the outside. For larger projects, such as Winter Fest Table Runner (page 17), I baste a grid every 3" or so.

I have a hard time using a thimble, so I usually end up with sore fingers. Sometimes I'll use one of the stick-on "thimbles," and that works well for me. I think the most important thing is to enjoy the process and not get too caught up in the technical aspects.

Tracing the Design

When it comes to tracing or transferring the embroidery design onto your fabric, I recommend using a light box. Start by pressing the waxy side of a piece of freezer paper to the wrong side of the fabric. The freezer paper will stabilize the fabric and make tracing easier. Tape the design in place on the light box, and then center the fabric on top of the design and secure it in place. I like to use a Pilot FriXion pen to trace lightly over the design. (The ink in a Pilot FriXion pen will disappear with the heat of an iron.) A fine-point washable marker, a ceramic pencil, or a mechanical or wooden pencil with a fine, hard lead will also work. When tracing onto a dark fabric, a white chalk pencil works well.

If you don't have a light box, you can tape the design to a window or use a glass-topped table with a lamp underneath.

About the Fabric

One of my favorite background fabrics for embroidery is Moda Crackle. It has a subtle design that creates a lovely texture next to the embroidery stitches. I used this for the background of most of the projects in this book.

Needles

I'm often asked what kind of needle I use for embroidery. There are many types of hand-sewing needles, each designed for a different technique. Needle packages are labeled by type and size. The larger the needle size, the smaller the needle (a size 1 needle will be longer and thicker than a size 12 needle). An embroidery needle is similar to a Sharp, but with an elongated eye designed to accommodate six-strand floss or pearl cotton. You may want to try a size 7, 8, or 9. To be honest, for me the eye of the needle just needs to be big enough to thread!

Hoops

Embroidery hoops are used to keep the fabric taut, but not tight, while stitching. Hoops are available in wood, metal, and plastic, with different mechanisms for keeping the fabric taut. Any type of hoop is fine, so take the time to find one you're comfortable with. I don't use a hoop, but if you'd like to use one I suggest trying a hoop that is 4", 5", or 6" in diameter to see what you prefer. Remember to always remove your fabric from the hoop when you've finished stitching for the day.

Embroidery Floss

All of the projects in this book were stitched using two strands of Cosmo floss unless otherwise noted. The conversion chart below will give you an approximate match to DMC floss. A few of the Cosmo flosses that I used are variegated. The projects will have a different look if stitched in a solid-color DMC floss.

COLOR	COSMO FLOSS	DMC FLOSS
Black	600	310
Brown	311	938
Dark gray-blue	894	645
Dark green	686	731
Ecru	1000	Ecru
Gold	775A	869
Medium blue-gray	892	647
Orange	129	976
Red	467	3777
Variegated gold-brown	8037	830
Variegated light blue	8049	642
Variegated light green	5012	3011

Resources

Ackfeld Wire Stand
Available at craft stores or online:
AckfeldWire.com
For the Giving Tree Tabletop Hanging on page 64, I used item #25207 with the snowflake header #34552.

Cord maker
KathySchmitz.com

Cosmos Floss
Happiness Is . . . Quilting
HappinessIsQuilting.com

Dunroven House Kitchen Towels
Miller's Dry Goods
4500 State Route 557
Millersburg, OH 44654
MillersDryGoods.com

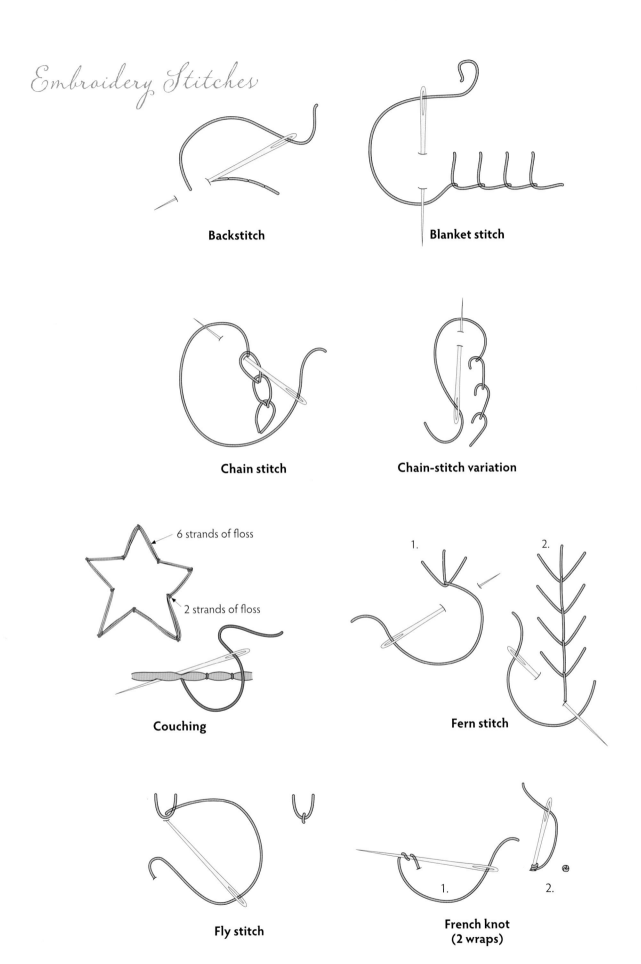

Backstitch

Blanket stitch

Chain stitch

Chain-stitch variation

6 strands of floss

2 strands of floss

Couching

1.

2.

Fern stitch

Fly stitch

1.

2.

**French knot
(2 wraps)**

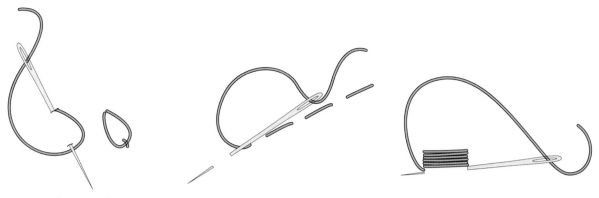

Lazy daisy stitch   **Running stitch**   **Satin stitch**

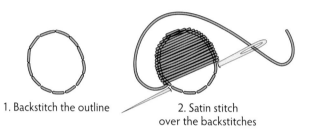

1. Backstitch the outline   2. Satin stitch over the backstitches

Satin-stitched circles

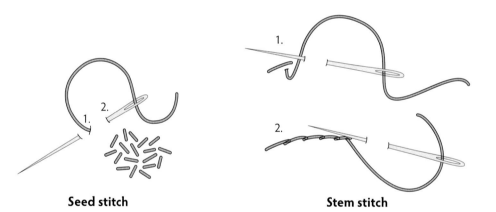

Seed stitch   **Stem stitch**

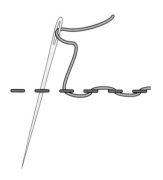

Straight stitch   **Whipped running stitch**

Cord Making

Adding a simple handmade twisted cord to cover seams or to add a color accent can turn a sweet little project into a classic treasure. Some of the projects in this book are finished using cording made from six strands of floss and a cord maker. Using a cord maker is relatively easy and lots of fun.

1 Cut a length of floss following the project instructions. (Each project lists the length of floss needed to make your cording. The ratio of floss to finished cording is about 5:1.)

2 Tie the ends together to form a large loop. Place the knot end on the hook of the cord maker (fig. 1).

3 Attach the loop end of the floss to a hook or other stationary object and start winding. It's very important to keep the floss taut while winding. Just keep going! Remember, you must keep constant tension on the floss.

4 Do the "kink test" by keeping the cording taut and *slowly* bringing it closer to the hook on the cord maker. If the cording kinks and twists together, it's ready (fig. 3).

5 Keeping the cording taut, remove the end of the cording from the cord maker. Place the hook of the cord maker over the cording at about the center of its length. Keeping a grip on the cord maker, bring the two ends of the cording together with your other hand. Remove the other end from the teacup hook. Hold both ends in one hand, with the ends pinched together, and hold the cord maker in the other hand.

6 Let go of the cord maker and let it spin and spin! When it stops spinning in one direction, remove it from the cording before it starts spinning in the opposite direction. Tie a knot at the ends you're holding (fig. 4).

Cording Tip

I make cording so often, I decided to screw a teacup hook into the side of my bookcase.

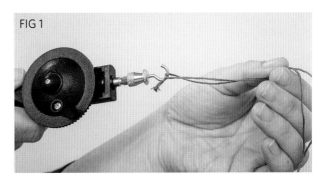

FIG 1

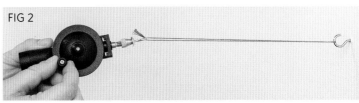

FIG 2

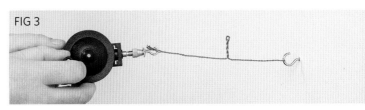

FIG 3

FIG 4

About the Author

When Kathy Schmitz was growing up, her mom always made sure that she and her sisters had an abundance of creative craft supplies at their fingertips. The girls were encouraged to draw and sew to their hearts' content, and many of their masterpieces were taped to the walls of their mom's sewing room. Kathy knew from a young age that *this* was what she wanted to do for a living! After many trials and errors, and jobs at banks and the like, Kathy says she is lucky enough to be what she always dreamed of being as a little girl—a designer. Kathy has designed fabric for Moda since 2002 and has had her own pattern company since 2007. Put a needle and thread or pen and ink in her hand, and she's a happy camper!

Kathy lives in beautiful Portland, Oregon, with her sweet hubby, Steve. Although her sons are grown and on their own, they are always close to her heart.